APRIL

S	1	8	15	22	29
M	2	9	16	23	30
Tu	3	10	17	24	
W	4	11	18	25	
Th	5	12	19	26	
F	6	13	20	27	
S	7	14	21	28	

MAY

S		6	13	20	27
M		7	14	21	28
Tu	1	8	15	22	29
W	2	9	16	23	30
Th	3	10	17	24	31
F	4	11	18	25	
S	5	12	19	26	

JUNE

S		3	10	17	24
M		4	11	18	25
Tu		5	12	19	26
W		6	13	20	27
Th		7	14	21	28
F	1	8	15	22	29
S	2	9	16	23	30

CONTENTS

The
Fireside Book

A picture and a poem
for every mood
chosen by

David Hope

Printed and published by
D.C. THOMSON & CO., LTD.,
185 Fleet Street, LONDON EC4A 2HS.
© D.C. Thomson & Co., Ltd., 2000.
ISBN 0 85116 738 1

SNOW IN SPRING

A LEADEN sky
  And snowflakes falling,
Sifting down through tender green.
Yet the earth is warm and vibrant,
Not for long this dazzling screen.

Where the wayward wind is blowing
Daffodils snow-laden lean,
Snowflakes whirling, falling, swirling.
Whitening where all was green.

P. M. Mayfield

A BUTTERFLY

ALL Winter the tortoiseshell had slept in the cupboard's dark;
Two folded halves, like a child's hands in prayer.
Now, with the new year melting,
With the daffodils buttering the field
And a great scythe of sunlight glancing across the valley
She awoke.

The blue embroidered edges of her wings
Tipped on the window-sill.
She fluttered against the glass like petals;
I put out one trembling finger and she climbed aboard,
No heavier than a dead leaf in Autumn.

The sun swam through our world again
And I scraped open the window
Held out the tortoiseshell till she lifted into April,
The start of her journey,
The one Summer of her flight.

Kenneth C. Steven

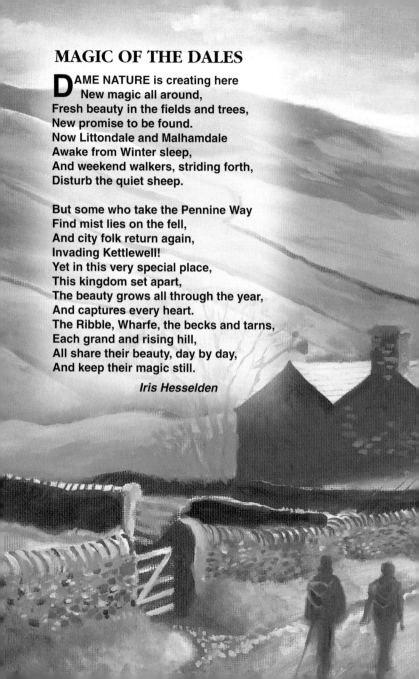

MAGIC OF THE DALES

DAME NATURE is creating here
   New magic all around,
Fresh beauty in the fields and trees,
New promise to be found.
Now Littondale and Malhamdale
Awake from Winter sleep,
And weekend walkers, striding forth,
Disturb the quiet sheep.

But some who take the Pennine Way
Find mist lies on the fell,
And city folk return again,
Invading Kettlewell!
Yet in this very special place,
This kingdom set apart,
The beauty grows all through the year,
And captures every heart.
The Ribble, Wharfe, the becks and tarns,
Each grand and rising hill,
All share their beauty, day by day,
And keep their magic still.

Iris Hesselden

CUPBOARD LOVE . . .

WHAT are her secret thoughts
  Behind those guileless eyes,
That graceful stretch of curving paw,
Those velvet pads that hide each claw,
These purrs that now arise?

What does she think of me,
When staring, as cats do
With measured and appraising glance,
She springs as though by sudden chance
Upon my lap to mew?

Does pussy really care,
Or is it just the chime
That tells the hour — a signal for
Her exit to the kitchen door
To hint it's supper-time?

Elizabeth Gozney

REFLECTIONS

WHICH is the mirror image?
Which is for true?
Each shawled in trailing wisps of shadow —
Blue green, green blue.
Mountains split by hairline streak —
A slash of yellow sand,
Double vision, upside-down on sea,
Down side up on land.
A cormorant flaps lazy wings,
Splinters the looking-glass bay.
A seal's head rises silkily in triumph
Mouthing sudden prey,
As seagulls plummet towards new-spied goal —
A small share in the seething shoal.

Anne Leask

SPRING WORSHIP

A CHOIR of praise
    In the bird-black trees,
And a sky of praying-blue.
A time of calm and quietude,
When peace moves down
The green-aisled lanes,
And hope strolls close behind.
Like white-robed hosts,
The surplice clouds sing
Mist-scored anthems sweet,
And pious hills exalt the sun
With psalms of budded life.
May-incense fills the holy air,
And, in the silver-plated pools,
Coined hymns ring Bible-true.

Glynfab John

S-S-S-SPIDERS

MARY says I make her laff
   Regarding spiders in the baff.
I know I leave the plughole plugged
In efforts to remain unbugged.
They still appear, no matter what.
If I could, I'd bomb the lot. ·

They're in the corners, on the stair.
The blooming things are everywhere.
If my courage I can muster,
I catch them in a yellow duster,
But only if their legs are short.
I can't abide the other sort.

I chase them with a tickling stick.
How they scuttle — quick, quick, quick.
They find escape routes everywhere.
They vanish, but I know they're there.

All windows closed to keep them out,
And so they climb right up the spout.
I hope they're hopping mad to find
The plughole plugged with them in mind.

Let them shove with all their might,
The bath remains stoppered tight,
And should they win with giant push,
I send them back with mighty scoosh.
They simply curl up small and float,
Survivors all, the loathsome lot.

Go away and play with Mary,
Especially if you're big and hairy.
That'll teach her not to laff
At me and spiders in the baff.

Katherine S. White

PRESTON MILL

THE mill stands poised
Like a fashion model,
Displaying tones and textures
From Nature's Collection.

Red pantiles drape the roof
With Madras cloth checks;
Cornerstones seam sandstone walls
In shades of sorrel;
A skirt of grass borders the buildings
In a lush green velvet
Polka-dotted with ducks.

A lamé pond shines like sequins in sun,
Its silver surface slubbed
With the wake of waterfowl.

The millwheel bobbin
Purls water from the stream;
White cotton yarn unravels
From every paddle.

Beyond the drawn-thread fence,
Is the corduroy of ploughed fields:
Light and shadow ruffle the nap
Into ripples of russet and chestnut.

Above, doves are appliquéd
On sky's azure bunting,
Pin feathers pointing to Phantassie
And dreams.

Rowena M. Love.

SPRING-SONG

THE trees are shrill
   With singing birds,
And black with budding nests;
The playful clouds
Blindfold the sun,
And tease the unveiled blue;
The meadows bleat
With flowering lambs,
Which blossomed overnight;
The perfumed breeze,
With feathered touch, bursts
Through the thin-skinned air;
Ploughed fields,
Like corrugated-cardboard lie,
And celandines,
Like golden stars, shine
In their grass-green sky;
The Spring-cleaned world's
A fresh-leaved dream —
Time's just an ivied myth!

Glynfab John

INTERLUDE

IT is late April on Holl Water.
  The rowan nipples have waited
The whole cold Spring to leaf
And pines are fixed, like picture mounts,
On fringes; for lack of foil they grieve.

In a muted motorboat, two fishers
Play out, play in their strings
To some untutored rite,
Buoyant as corks, adrift,
Long careless of time or light.

A second boat plashes its oars
Without direction, with no depth
— An old man counting the total
Sum of his life and breaking even.
With a single coot at full throttle

The only life pursuing life
And wisps of mist now elvering
Across the water, we are marooned
In microcosm. Save
For the stretching shadow of West Lomond.

Ian Nimmo White

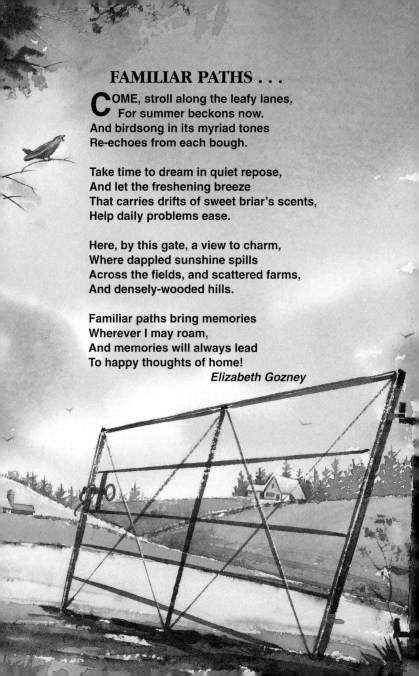

FAMILIAR PATHS . . .

COME, stroll along the leafy lanes,
   For summer beckons now.
And birdsong in its myriad tones
Re-echoes from each bough.

Take time to dream in quiet repose,
And let the freshening breeze
That carries drifts of sweet briar's scents,
Help daily problems ease.

Here, by this gate, a view to charm,
Where dappled sunshine spills
Across the fields, and scattered farms,
And densely-wooded hills.

Familiar paths bring memories
Wherever I may roam,
And memories will always lead
To happy thoughts of home!

Elizabeth Gozney

POPPIES

WHERE clover nestles, rich and nectar-blessed,
  Among the murmuring wayside wilderness,
A blaze of blood-bright poppies
Sprang to flame,
Vibrant and sweet as new-found happiness.

Dimming the blushing sorrel's rosy warmth,
Melting the foam-cool clouds of meadowsweet,
Like fronds of fire they glimmered through
The green
And fell, a shower of sparks, among the wheat.

Joan Howes

HERO

WHO'S my best chum?
Grandpa, for sure.

See him on my skateboard!
He's ace.
Computer games? No bother to Gramps.
He can cook, too. Sticky toffee pudding
Is his favourite. Mine, too.

He never asks, "Have you washed your neck,
Made your bed, changed your socks?"
I like going to his house.

"Daft as a brush," my mum calls him
As we chase a ball around the park
And oh, how she goes on about the junk
He collects in his shed.
But you should see the things he makes!
Kites, a sledge, a scarecrow
And a smashing thing on old pram wheels
He calls a cairtie.

"Grandpa's ace," I tell Mum.
She nods and says, "Yes, son,
But that was a long time ago,
During the war,
When he was flying Spitfires."

Funny he never speaks about that.
Probably has more important things
On his mind, like going fishing
With me, his best chum.

Silvie Taylor

BEES

IN Winter, while the days sting white with cold,
And all the hills are glazed,
We forget them.

Then one day, without a warning,
As if the earth has tilted into light,
The birds awaken and the land is gold.

Till out of nowhere the bees hum, tawny
Drizzle through the flowers, motorway the air,
Rumble on the inside of our windows.

They are like the drones of bagpipes
Furry things that carry in their wings
A thousand flights of pollen.

Strange that all their lives
Should be homogenised, a weight of journeys
Made sweet and pure as honey.

Kenneth C. Steven

JUNE HEATWAVE

TINDER-DRY, burned to brown
By the scorching June sun,
The stubble stiffly stands
Where field-mice used to run.

In barn and in rick now,
Securely hived away,
Sweetly smells the harvest
Of honey-scented hay.

Noon's hazy heat veils
The features of every hill,
And the loveliest haunts
Of enchantment are still.

Shimmering meadows slumber,
In hedgerows no birds sing,
And silence lulls to sleep
Each drowsy living thing.

Glynfab John

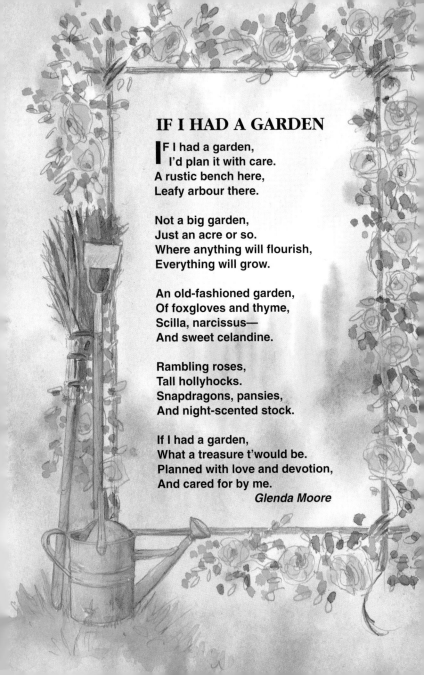

IF I HAD A GARDEN

IF I had a garden,
  I'd plan it with care.
A rustic bench here,
Leafy arbour there.

Not a big garden,
Just an acre or so.
Where anything will flourish,
Everything will grow.

An old-fashioned garden,
Of foxgloves and thyme,
Scilla, narcissus—
And sweet celandine.

Rambling roses,
Tall hollyhocks.
Snapdragons, pansies,
And night-scented stock.

If I had a garden,
What a treasure t'would be.
Planned with love and devotion,
And cared for by me.

Glenda Moore

THIS QUIET REFLECTION

THE radiance of the setting sun
   Is beauty to behold,
It gilds majestic, rising cliffs
In hues of flame and gold.

Its slanting beams illuminate
A pathway o'er the sea,
Contrasting with the darkening shore
In quiet serenity.

This timeless hour to gather strength
As swiftly fades the light;
The purple shadows blend and merge
To cloak encroaching night . . .

Elizabeth Gozney

THE SHEPHERD'S TREE

HUGE elm, with rifted trunk all notched and scarred,
  Like to a warrior's destiny, I love
To stretch me often on thy shadowed sward,
And hear the laugh of summer leaves above;
Or on thy buttressed roots to sit, and lean
In careless attitude, and there reflect
On times and deeds and darings that have been —
Old castaways, now swallowed in neglect —
While thou art towering in thy strength of heart,
Stirring the soul to vain imaginings
In which life's sordid being hath no part.
The wind of that eternal ditty sings,
Humming of future things, that burn the mind
To leave some fragment of itself behind.

                                        John Clare

THE LACQUERED BOX

I HAVE a box; tis very old,
  Silk-lined and lacquered, blue and gold.
Of quaint design and beauty rare,
It guards my treasures none may share.

A photograph, now turning brown;
A fragment from a wedding gown;
A letter, written from the heart,
By one who knew we had to part.

A lock of hair, of sunny hue;
A ribbon of the palest blue;
A flower pressed in a tiny book,
So fragile that I scarce dare look.

A drawing by my sister's boy;
A battered but once well-loved toy;
A golden ring, its stone a-glow;
A poem sent me long ago.
My treasures call back days of yore;
I simply could not love them more.
Within that box, to me it seems,
Lie safely all my dearest dreams.

Peter Cliffe

CORNISH LANDSCAPE

ATLANTIC wind across Land's End
   Sweeps in with early rain,
Grey mist creeps up the moorland road
Where old tin mines remain.
Mysterious and mystical,
A special atmosphere,
As ancient standing stones reveal
The magic lingers here.

But soon the wind blows fresher still
And drives away the clouds,
Bright sunlight sparkles on the sea
To welcome Summer crowds.
In Penzance town the traffic grows,
Another busy day,
St Michael's Mount lies bathed in peace,
Another world away.

From Newquay sands to Lizard Point
That special feeling starts,
It reaches out across the miles
And lives on in our hearts.

Iris Hesselden

MUSIC OF THE TREES

DOWN by the boathouse the reeds stir,
  A gentle murmur on the breeze.
The pines reach almost to the water's edge,
And sunlight dapples them.
Warm pebbles on the beach await
The cooling Summer rain.

It comes, and the music of the trees begins,
Sighs through the forest,
Breathes an anthem, echoing
Cathedral-high.
Cascading drops cascade their way
From branch to branch
With all the crystal clarity of
A pure voice singing.

Katherine S. White

DAHLIA "ARABIAN NIGHT" AT WAKEHURST

BACKED by a tall and weathered wall they stand,
Exotics in a wind-blown sanguine band,
That velvet-plush allusive name just right:
— Bedouin welcome, dark empurpled night —
Or Vulcan's pie-frills deftly hammered crisp
To discs like faces tinged by ferrous mist.

Observe the yellow seed-bed at the heart —
A dewy cushion-couch of nature's art;
Forget not thrusting root or polished stem,
The calyx like some greenish diadem;
Note the leaf-shape, gaze at giddy length,
From such throbbing resonance draw strength.

O dusky queens Autumnal yet serene,
Transformed by man to feed his ardent dream
Of burgeonings that seem to sing and sound,
A paradise at Wakehurst have I found
Where bee and worm their roles supporting play,
And dahlias in my mind shall bedded stay.

Diana Dykes

DRAGONFLIES

THE first time I saw them I was only ten;
  I had struggled half an hour through heather
To the round brooch of that hill loch.
It was June, sunlight hot on every stone and hollow;
I wanted home to the dark cool of the corridors,
A hiding place and a book.
Then all at once I saw the dragonflies, like silent helicopters,
Their gauze wings thin and brittle
As the windows of a Chinese lantern.
Low they steered over pools and reed beds
The blue of their bodies bold
As the splash on a kingfisher's breast.
But when suddenly I got up, mad to catch one,
Lumbered clumsily and loudly over boulders,
They vanished in a breath, soft as the breeze,
Drifted into the distance like blue thread.

Kenneth C. Steven

AYRSHIRE COAST, LATE SUMMER

THE sands of time trickle to late Summer.
Off-season approaches:
The empty bed of beach tucked up for Winter.

Soon, the shore will be piled high
With Ayrshire blankets of sand,
Rumpled by a receding tide;
At its height, watered-silk sheets will spread slickly
To dunes' lumpy pillows,
Surf trimming them thickly with lace.

Awaiting the Autumn,
The sleeping warrior snuggles
Beneath his duvet of rosy pink clouds;
Eiderdown feathers fluttering free
To fly south.

But Winter isn't here yet:
Overtired youngsters rub sleep from their eyes,
Demanding one last game
Before the Sandman comes.

Rowena M. Love

JACK-BY-THE-HEDGE

OLD snow-capped straggler
  Craning above the froth of parsley heads.
Spindly wayside loiterer
Stretching thin stalks
And heart-shaped leaves
Over the rosy stars of campion.

Where grasses mingle and old ivies cling
Close to the dew-wet soil,
Your aspiration lifts you clear
Of tangled leaf and root.
Skinny and uninspiring you might seem,
Yet your straight stem outstrips
The elbowing mass below.

No dock or dandelion for your bedfellows.
The budding dog-rose
Hangs within your reach
And elderflowers shake their petals down
To brush your eager leaves
With creamy dust.

Joan Howes

A POEM FOR ANN

THREE feet small
  With dreams as big as Christmas.

A cornfield of curls
And a smile that would melt a soldier.

When you cry
All of you falls to pieces;
Everyone comes running to mend you.

At night your eyes look huge;
You are afraid of the owl
That ghosts your bedroom window.

I tell you a story
But you are kingdoms and princes away
Long before the ending.

In the morning I will bring you blackbirds
And put the sun on your pillow.
I will tie your laces,
And pray safe roads for your feet.

Kenneth C. Steven

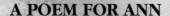

THESE THINGS I LOVE

I LOVE to see dawn's blushing hue
   Tint heaven's face, and pass;
I love to see the pearls of dew
Enrich a sea of grass.

I love a valley bathed in light,
Fanned by the breezy day
Sweeping away the veil of night,
To let the sunbeams play.

I love soft, balmy morning air,
The crowing of the cocks;
I love green fields where shepherds care
For docile, fleecy flocks.

I love chaste daisies, virgin-white,
Starred in the upland lawn;
I love proud poppies, red and bright,
That mingle with the corn.

Yes, I love thunder and the rain
That falls upon the earth;
I love the spasms of stormy pain
When pregnant clouds give birth.

I love a peaceful, grey churchyard,
Where ancient yew trees stand,
Like sentinels destined to guard
The consecrated land.

I love to watch the sun sink deep
Behind the hilltop's rim,
Then offer up, before I sleep,
My quiet bedtime hymn.

Glynfab John

JUST PURR-FECT!

WOULD that I, a genius be,
  To capture for posterity,
The dreams and visions of the mind,
A masterpiece in oils, designed
To fill the eye with endless bliss,
And hear the crowds say, "Look at this!"
To see the critics stand and stare,
And feel the homage in the air;
To know by my unerring hand,
The jumbled thoughts, ideas I'd planned,
Were now transferred to canvas, by
My canny brush, and steady eye!
Alas! My own artistic flair
Describes "home grown", and can't compare,
And puss, my critic, fails to bow —
Though graciously concedes, "Miaow!" . . .

Elizabeth Gozney.

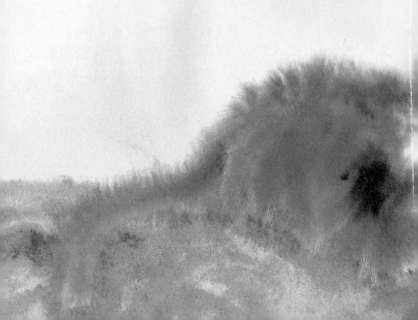

NIGHT JOURNEY

AS I ride alone on the midnight trail,
  While the stars shine bright and the moon's a-sail,
The pinto's hooves and the wind's sad song
Are the sounds I hear as I go along.

Something ahead makes the pony shy;
It comes with a rush; as it races by
I reach for my gun; but there ain't no need,
For the ghostly thing is a tumbleweed.

I pass a cactus as tall as a man:
Must have been there since the world began!
From far away, where the old hills rise,
Like a lonely spirit a coyote cries.

I long for day and the sun above;
For the welcoming smile of the girl I love.
Then a hoot-owl calls as the moon goes down,
And I see in the distance the lights of town.

In the eastern sky is the gleam of dawn,
And I whistle a tune as I travel on,
For night has ended, the ranch shows plain,
I'm almost home and I'm happy again.

Peter Cliffe

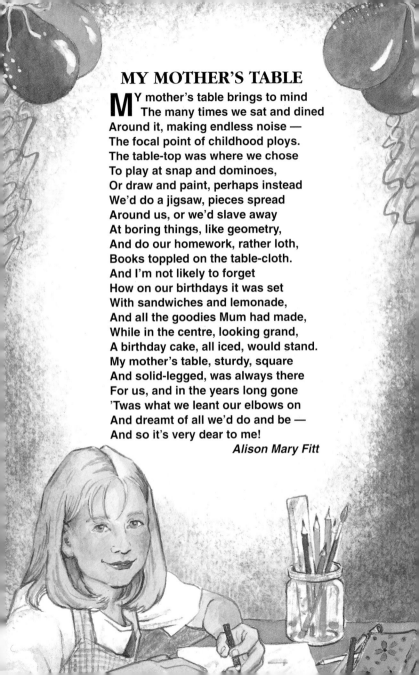

MY MOTHER'S TABLE

MY mother's table brings to mind
    The many times we sat and dined
Around it, making endless noise —
The focal point of childhood ploys.
The table-top was where we chose
To play at snap and dominoes,
Or draw and paint, perhaps instead
We'd do a jigsaw, pieces spread
Around us, or we'd slave away
At boring things, like geometry,
And do our homework, rather loth,
Books toppled on the table-cloth.
And I'm not likely to forget
How on our birthdays it was set
With sandwiches and lemonade,
And all the goodies Mum had made,
While in the centre, looking grand,
A birthday cake, all iced, would stand.
My mother's table, sturdy, square
And solid-legged, was always there
For us, and in the years long gone
'Twas what we leant our elbows on
And dreamt of all we'd do and be —
And so it's very dear to me!

Alison Mary Fitt

ARGYLL

ALL down the coast
  The air was full of fish and sunset.

By nine the lemon-coloured cottages
Were warm windows glowing over the bays.

Far west the light a rim of blue and white,
Jura and Mull and Scarba all carved from shining.

On the way home we stopped to listen to the dark,
To the sea coming huge over a hundred beaches.

In among the trees, in windless stillness,
The bats were flitting, weaving patterns with the air.

That night I did not want the stars to rise at all
I wanted it to be like this and nothing more

Looking west into the sunset
To the very end of the world.

Kenneth C. Steven

KESWICK EVENING

THE dusk came creeping, silently,
The rain came sweeping down,
But lights shone out in Keswick streets,
A welcome to the town.
The visitors were blown around,
And buffeted along,
And Derwentwater lost its calm
As teasing winds grew strong.

The gutters ran like mountain streams,
And cars caused drenching spray,
Returning walkers laughed and joked,
And nothing spoiled their day.
More lights shone out in hostelries,
More thoughts of food and wine!
And who knows what tomorrow brings?
Tomorrow may be fine!

Iris Hesselden

TAKE ME BACK

TAKE me back,
  Oh, take me back,
To the hills
Which once I knew;
Where softly sighed
The scented breeze,
And wild, wild flowers grew;
Where high-pitched larks,
Up, up above,
Pin-pricked the sky
With song;
Where all the paths
Seemed steeple-steep
When my young legs
Felt strong;
Where Summer days
Were far too short,
The bracken, guardsman-tall;
And yew trees stood
Like sentinels
Within the churchyard wall.

Glynfab John

NIGHTFALL

THE moon comes up
　　An expectant pizza crust
And darkness falls
A charcoal cloak
Enveloping the God-like glow of sunshine
Fading, as it slips silently
Down the far side of the hills
To dunk in the mysterious loch below.

Puffed-out monsters billow by
Echoed thoughts broken
By inklings of twilight
Watched by startled stars
As they play hide-and-seek
Behind the dull grey clouds
And twinkle
In the sea of darkling indigo.
Their joy is eternal.

Kendric Ross

HOMECOMING

I STROLL along the platform
  As the train moves out of sight,
And breathe the Summer's essence
In the evening's golden light,
While the windmill sails keep turning,
Turning far away,
And I am coming home again,
Home again to stay . . .

The cottage gardens beckon,
And the children shout and cheer,
The old folk wave a greeting,
As I brush away a tear;
And the windmill sails keep turning
Turning on their way,
And I am nearing home again,
Home at last, to stay . . .

Elizabeth Gozney

SEPTEMBER SONG

IN the mists of Autumn mornings,
  Summer dreams seem swift to fade,
As the chill of colder dawnings
Lightly frosts each grassy blade.
Yet for all we grieve the passing
Of those warm and gentle days,
Who could not rejoice in seeing
Autumn's glory start to blaze?
Who would not admire her brushstrokes,
Skilled in perfect artistry,
Painting now, with vivid brilliance,
Every leaf on every tree.
Tinting pears and gilding apples
Yellow as a honeycomb.
Autumn, in her bounteous beauty,
Shares her gifts of harvest home.

Margaret Ingall

LOVE AT FIRST SIGHT?

A FROG has not the kind of face
We would associate with grace.
Although he sees his type of looks
Reflecting well in babbling brooks;
And true, he is the gardener's friend
Whose cabbage patch, he will defend.
And rather to our great surprise
His bulbous, sad-looking eyes,
Now start to sparkle, bright and keen
When lady frog leaps on the scene!
And though she'd win no beauty stakes,
She obviously an impact makes;
Which prompts an age-cold cliché's whim —
Whatever does she see in him . . .?

Elizabeth Gozney

THE SLOW WAVE

THE slow wave curls, and crashes
Upon the passive sand:
A crowd of creamy fleeces
Whose journey never ceases
Prance all along the beaches
And die into the land.

The small waves chucklebubble,
The big waves thunderlaugh;
They gather height, they quiver
And poise and, breaking, shiver
And spread, cream, laced with silver —
Repentant after wrath?

That living scroll of water,
Unrolling endlessly,
Contains unwritten histories,
Conceals forgotten mysteries,
Hints at the hidden witcheries
And magic of the sea.

R. L. Cook

SEAS AND NOTIONS

THRU' centuries Salts have sailed,
O'er boisterous Biscay Bay,
East, the tideless Med
And down the Red.
West on broad Atlantic
To Carib's pearl-strung islands.

Beyond Panama, beckons the Pacific still,
As it did Van Diemen, Cook and Drake
On their watery odysseys
Cleaving its vastness.

All seas edit with their tides
Humankind's times and traffic.
Man's a mere vassal, his vessels pawns
Moving in and out and about
As Neptune, god of seas
Decrees.

Joe H. McGibbon

NOVEMBER NOCTURNE

A CHILL, unlovely dawn, trailing wet-shod
Into a cobweb morning, lost in haze.
Drab afternoon, dragging its laggard feet,
To blend, unmourned, among the evening greys.
Despite the gloom, excited undertones
Run like a whisper through the shrouded mire.
Swift, eager footsteps dare the darkling time
When twilight warms its fingers at the fire.
Dismal November wears its glory well
For this bright hour of treason's brief acclaim.
The splintered sky bursts into founts of light
As guys, in star-splashed gardens, die aflame.

Joan Howes

MANY MOONS AGO

CYCLING up to Burnsall,
Many moons ago,
Leaving Leeds and Bradford,
Many miles to go.
Making camp at Drebley,
Great to be a Scout,
Sleeping by the River Wharfe
As the stars come out.

Waking in the darkness,
Listening to a noise,
Only cattle munching,
Nothing scares these boys.
Rising in the morning,
Rain comes lashing down,
Wishing we were warm and dry,
Safely back in town.
Cycling home from Burnsall,
Singing on our way,
Was it many moons ago
Or only yesterday?

Iris Hesselden

EVERYDAY THINGS

SEEK out the beauty
In everyday things,
Look at the patterns
On butterfly wings.
Birds, trees and flowers
The moon way up high,
Millions of diamonds
Strung out in the sky.
Seashells and sunbeams
A blackbird that sings,
Don't miss the beauty
In commonplace things.

Kathleen Gillum

THE STANDING STONE

TALL, rough stone
   Gaunt finger pointing to the sky
Who raised you here? And why?
Upon this spot

No carving shown
To mark a sacred burial ground
Nor trace the lunar passage round
Or tribal plot

You stand alone
A record from the mists of time
Ravaged by sun and frosty rime
Remembered not

By moss o'ergrown
But still with dignity and grace
Evoke in us a sense of place
A passing thought

That yet unknown
We too may make our mark
A beacon shining in the dark
As so we ought.

Earle Douglas

THE HILLS

STANDING proud against the azure sky
How humble do we feel?
Walking amidst their mighty shapes
Is awesome — ever real.
The crags, the glens, the forest path
The sunlight through the tree
The Lord He gave us these great things
For all of us to see.
The waterfall comes tumbling down
Amongst the forest glade
Cascading onwards from its source
Through channels it has made.
The sunset on the mighty hills
What wondrous sights to see
The purple shadows painted there
God made for you and me.
To walk in wonder and in peace
In tranquil hills adore
Lift up your heart, lift up your voice
And thank God evermore.

Ian L. Fyfe

FIRESIDE BLESSINGS

CURTAINS drawn on a Winter's night
Hot buttered toast for tea.
My family gathered round the fire,
A treasured time for me.

The warm soft light of candles,
The crimson firelight glow.
A haven from the outside world,
A world of drifting snow.

The baby stirs upon my knee,
His little hand curled tight.
A wealth of love envelops me,
And fills my heart tonight.

I count my blessings once again,
As I so often do,
And glance across to where you sit,
I owe it all to you.

Maureen Anne Cooper

FROM 'FROST AT MIDNIGHT"

THEREFORE all seasons shall be sweet to thee,
   Whether the Summer clothe the general earth
With greenness, or the redbreast sit and sing
Betwixt the tufts of snow on the bare branch
Of mossy apple-tree, while the night thatch
Smokes in the sun-thaw; whether the eave-drops fall
Heard only in the trances of the blast,
Or if the secret ministry of frost
Shall hang them up in silent icicles,
Quietly shining to the quiet moon.

Samuel Taylor Coleridge

YORKSHIRE
TRAVELLER

SITTING in my armchair,
  hear the cold wind blow,
See the weather forecast,
  promising more snow.
Close the curtains tightly,
  leave the world outside,
Then I travel nightly,
  memories my guide.
Climb the hill to Haworth,
  walk across the moor,
Take the path the Brontës
  trod many years before.
See the Summer sunshine
  light the Yorkshire dales,
On the banks of Wharfe and Nidd,
  hear those fishing tales!
Sitting in my armchair,
  Yorkshire in my heart,
Memories of Yorkshire pud.,
  thoughts of treacle tart.
Climb the slopes of Whernside,
  watch the sun arise,
Count the stars from Pen-y-Ghent
  as the daylight dies.
Sights and sounds surround me,
  sitting in my chair,
Travelling through Yorkshire,
  wishing I was there!

Iris Hesselden

WHITE SPIRIT WINTER

DARK clouds stencil images
On a Winter sky's pale emulsion.

Rain glosses dead branches;
Pushes back the protective sheet of snow,
Revealing a residue of rotting
Paint flake leaves.

Stripper has been brushed
Over the grey primer of tree trunks
Until they bubble with lichen.

Nature dabbles with special effects:
The distressed wood of peeling bark;
Mock verdigris on north-facing boughs;
Rag-rolled streams.

Waterfalls of white spirit
Clean Winter's palette,
So all is in readiness
For a fresh coat

Of leaves.

Rowena M. Love

WINTER STILLNESS

SNOW lies soft and silent
  Over the cold earth,
Turned to lavender
Under a crescent moon.

Fields are hushed,
Locked in Winter's waiting time.
Shy trees cannot hide
Their crystal beauty.

The road to home winds ahead,
Marked only by
The wandering
Fence.

Snow creaks under my boots,
And the sound
Cracks across the silence
Like rifle shot.

Katherine S. White

BIRDS IN WINTER

HIGH o'er the restless deep, above the reach
   Of gunner's hope, vast flights of wild ducks stretch;
Far as the eye can glance on either side,
In a broad space and level line they glide;
All in their wedge-like figures from the north,
Day after day, flight after flight, go forth.
In-shore, their passage tribes of sea-gulls urge
And drop for prey within the sweeping surge;
Oft in the rough opposing blast they fly
Far back, then turn, and all their force apply,
While to the storm they give their weak complaining cry,
Or clap the sleek white pinion to the breast,
And in the restless ocean dip for rest.

George Crabbe

The artists are:—

Pat Bray; This Quiet Reflection.
Sheila Carmichael; Snow In Spring,
Spring-Song, September Song,
Everyday Things.
Jackie Cartwright;
My Mother's Table.
John Dugan; Music Of The Trees,
Seas And Notions, November
Nocturne, White Spirit Winter.
Alan Haldane; Poppies, These
Things I Love, The Standing Stone.
Eunice Harvey; A Butterfly,
Cupboard Love, Nightfall.
Harry McGregor; Cornish Land-
scape, Ayrshire Coast, Late
Summer, Winter Stillness.
Norma Maclean; The Lacquered
Box, Dragonflies, Jack-By-The-
Hedge,Fireside Blessings.
Sandy Milligan; Interlude, Night
Journey.
Keith Robson; Magic Of The Dales,
Spring Worship, Preston Mill,
The Shepherd's Tree, Keswick
Evening, Homecoming,
Many Moons Ago,Yorkshire Traveller.
Staff Artists; Reflections,
 S-S-S-Spiders, Familiar Paths,
Hero, Bees, June Heatwave,
If I Had A Garden, Dahlia "Arabian
Night" At Wakehurst, A Poem For
Ann, Just Purr-fect!, Argyll, Take Me
Back, Love At First Sight?, The Slow
Wave, The Hills, From 'Frost At
Midnight', Birds In Winter.

JULY

S	1	8	15	22	29
M	2	9	16	23	30
Tu	3	10	17	24	31
W	4	11	18	25	
Th	5	12	19	26	
F	6	13	20	27	
S	7	14	21	28	

AUGUST

S		5	12	19	26
M		6	13	20	27
Tu		7	14	21	28
W	1	8	15	22	29
Th	2	9	16	23	30
F	3	10	17	24	31
S	4	11	18	25	

SEPTEMBER

S		2	9	16	23	30
M		3	10	17	24	
Tu		4	11	18	25	
W		5	12	19	26	
Th		6	13	20	27	
F		7	14	21	28	
S	1	8	15	22	29	